The Collector's Guide To
BUTTONS

Janet Owen
215 Tanglewood Drive
Alexandria, LA 71303

The Collector's Guide To

BUTTONS

Diana Epstein

Walker and Company
New York

FRONTISPIECE: Two-part steel die, intaglio and raised halves, used to strike designs on metal buttons. Brass button with identical center as die, but no border design.

OPPOSITE: Hand-stamped late 18th century tombac sporting button.

First published in the United States of America in 1990 by Walker Publishing Company, Inc.

Published simultaneously in Canada by Thomas Allen & Son

Canada, Limited, Markham, Ontario
Library of Congress Cataloging-in-Publication Data

Epstein, Diana.
The collector's guide to buttons / Diana Epstein.
ISBN 0-8027-7342-7
1. Buttons—Collectors and collecting. I. Title.
NK3668.5.E67   1990
646'.19—dc20   90-12519
CIP

Printed in the United States of America

2   4   6   8   10   9   7   5   3   1

CENTURIES OF BUTTONS involve too many varieties, histories, and geographies to include them all in this small book. Buttons are here presented as chronologically as possible, and placed within their fashion and art, with button-collecting terminology left to books and publications written especially for collectors. Specialized button categories that are books in themselves—armed forces buttons, nonmilitary uniform buttons, and historical and political buttons—have been omitted.

Any button book must acknowledge the devoted early collectors for sharing their research and information and for taking buttons out of the family button box and into the museum. In particular, the author wishes to thank Mrs. Sally C. Luscomb for her encouragement and help with this book, her generous loans of buttons and photographs, and for her friendship and inspiration. Special thanks is due to Mr. Victor E. Luscomb for his assistance and confidence. The author is also grateful to Mrs. R. F. Halpin for lending many lovely eighteenth-century buttons and for her gracious cooperation. *The National Button Bulletin* and *Just Buttons* magazine have provided valuable reference material in connection with this volume.

ABOVE: Liverpool transfer buttons, English, mid- to late-19th century. The porcelain centers, mounted in metal, are decorated by attic-toned neo-classic transfer designs with handpainted accents.

OPPOSITE: Back of one-piece 18th century tombac button.

INTRODUCTION

TO HERALD A FAMOUS BUTTON or recite a fascinating button fact might winningly introduce the subject of buttons, but to meet a button in person is the surest captivation. Buttons are irresistible small relics, documents of art, craft, history, and legend. It is necessary to set aside the association of buttons as trifles, to revise their image as everyday fasteners, and to restore to them the importance, splendor, and exclusiveness that made them luxury items through the eighteenth century.

Buttons have a long and elegant history, and their value as art, as well as artifact, is increasing. The study of buttons includes a survey of every imaginable natural and created material, employing every art and craft in their manufacture, and an encyclopedic reflection of subjects and trends in their design. There are buttons of gold, precious jewels, ivory, porcelain, tortoiseshell, paper, potatoes, butterfly wings, and bird feathers. Button decoration includes enameling, etching, engraving, carving, *découpage*, stenciling, pyrography, weaving, needlework, and all manners of painting. In both materials and methods, this is to name a few; a more difficult task would be to name anything that cannot be found among buttons.

That there are extraordinary buttons surprises many, but that there are buttons, which are collected, surprises all but those who collect them. Although a relatively young hobby, button collecting could be considered the most cosmopolitan member of collecting society, including as it does the forms and fancies of nearly all other collectibles. In whatever family of collection, there is a button relative to join it, eligible to the same terminology and classification. For collectors of Wedgwood, Meissen, Satsuma, paperweights, Art Nouveau, pewter, and tintypes, there are buttons to add to their collections. Collectors of political campaign items can find candidates, symbols, and slogans on

OPPOSITE: 18th century buttons, all under glass, with metal rims. Clockwise (from the top): oil painting (signed Ramet); reverse painting on glass (possibly a reproduction); painting on ivory; ink drawing on paper; painting on ivory; colored print; printing on paper; watercolor. Center button with paper design and pressed paper mat.

buttons. Admirers of Kate Greenaway can compare her book illustrations with button copies. Accumulators of World's Fair memorabilia should include buttons made as souvenirs and those made to advertise and celebrate the fairs. Whether a collector's interest is grounded in bicycles or floating toward balloons, there are buttons which depict the styles and stages of development.

Buttons can also be an adjunct to interests outside the collection of antiques. Historians of the French Revolution could illustrate a history of that rebellion with appropriate eighteenth-century buttons. Fanciers of animals, minerals, or vegetables will find varieties of buttons picturing their favorite. There is a bee farmer with a collection of buttons relating to bees.

Not organized as a formal hobby in America until the late 1930's, buttons had traditionally been saved and passed from generation to generation as mementos and sentiments of the past. Both in America and abroad, the luxurious eighteenth-century buttons were saved as much for their intrinsic value as they were as art objects or souvenirs. Very few buttons are found pre-dating the eighteenth century, and most collectors concentrate their collections on buttons of the nineteenth century. As traveling button collectors unearth buttons from everywhere, as more books and magazines contain button lore, and as exhibits grow displaying rare and beautiful buttons, the focus of button collecting is expanding beyond local and regional finds and including earlier and more select items.

If you are looking for a wilderness to pioneer, buttons is still a frontier. Old-fashioned adventures such as exploring, digging, and discovering await button enthusiasts. There recently has been published an encyclopedia of buttons, there is a button museum in Connecticut, and The Metropolitan Museum of Art in New York City has acquired a rare private button collection (not yet on display). But there is still little information, few authorities or experts to teach and advise, and little source material on the subject.

In addition to providing an introductory framework and showcase for potential button collectors, this book presents buttons as artistic objects for everyone to appreciate. A special and additional fascination of buttons, particularly at a time when mass production and largeness are virtues, is their invitation to pause and concentrate on miniature and skillful pieces of handwork. In the mid-1800's Dickens wrote about buttons in *Household Words*: "There is surely something charming in seeing the smallest thing done so thoroughly, as if to remind the careless that whatever is worth doing is worth doing well."

Tombac buttons on a black wool coat, 18th century, Denmark.

CHAPTER I

Early Buttons

THERE IS NO EVIDENCE by whom, when, or where the first button was used. Unlike objects which have inventors or birthdates, and even unlike those, such as the sandwich, which have legendary origins, the button vaguely crops out from various histories without even an hieroglyphic clue to pinpoint it. The best sources for tracing earliest buttons are old costumes, costume histories, or clothing in engravings, paintings, and sculpture.

To date, the earliest button finds were made in excavations in Egypt, Greece, and Persia. These buttons—some as much as four thousand years old, made of materials such as gold, glass, bone, and earthenware—although constructed like buttons, were probably not used to fasten garments but as ornaments, seals, or badges.

In *The Influence of Invention on Civilization*, M. D. C. Crawford includes the button in a prodigious list of prehistoric inventions, crediting paleolithic man with originating buttons and toggles. In one of the earliest of the scant early references to buttons, in the middle of the thirteenth century, Étienne Boileau, Provost of Paris, established laws governing the guilds of French craftsmen, which included rules and penalties for buttonmakers.

More information is provided by costume histories and other records, which picture various clothing with buttonlike ornaments—including those that caught the flow of tunics and chitons of the Greeks and Etruscans, those closing the garments beneath a knight's armor in the Middle Ages, and the long rows that ornamented the fronts and sleeves of both men's and women's clothing of the Renaissance.

There are legends about, and pictorial evidence to confirm, opulent sixteenth- and seventeenth-century buttons worn by nobles and aristocrats. In the

OPPOSITE: Prehistoric buttons of pottery and stone, from excavations in Egypt. Although they have shanklike apertures, these early "buttons" were probably worn on cords or chains; intaglio designs may have been seals.

many diaries, accounts of toilette, and shop and household inventories from the seventeenth century, there are occasional enumerations of buttons or descriptions of buttons worn. Front and back openings of men's doublets, wrist openings, and slits in breeches were lavishly edged with buttons, as were the fronts of women's gowns and coats. More often these buttons were ornamental, or just a few buttoned. Seventeenth-century buttons, regardless of the great variety of national fashions, were largely fabric, decorated by needlework; but metal buttons were made also, and at the end of the last decade, men's coats began to blaze with diamond buttons.

Despite the obvious and increased use of buttons in the seventeenth century, button authorities and collectors largely have ignored buttons prior to the eighteenth century, dismissing them as chiefly decorative. Implicit in this attitude is the collectors' distinction that an authentic button must fulfill its primary dictionary definition as a fastener of clothing; however, the point is academic, since few if any of these early "buttons" have been found. Certainly for purposes of collecting, button lore begins with the rich and surprisingly numerous examples from the eighteenth century.

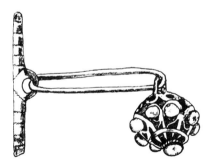

ABOVE: Toggle button. As early fasteners, toggle buttons were usually heavy silver, made in various European countries for centuries before the 17th century.

OPPOSITE: Lavishly buttoned 17th century French gentleman. Rows of buttons on sleeves, cuffs, outer and under coat fronts are largely decorative; few pre-18th century buttons were functional.

PAGE 16: Embroidered silk waistcoat, 18th century French, fabric-covered buttons embroidered to match. Courtesy of The Cooper Union Museum.

PLATE: 18th century French millinery fashions, from a set of paintings on ivory under glass, ca. 1775. The Metropolitan Museum of Art, Hanna S. Kohn Button Collection.

OPPOSITE: Print illustrating machines and hand tools for manufacturing various kinds of buttons.

BUTTON MAKING.

PLATE CVII.

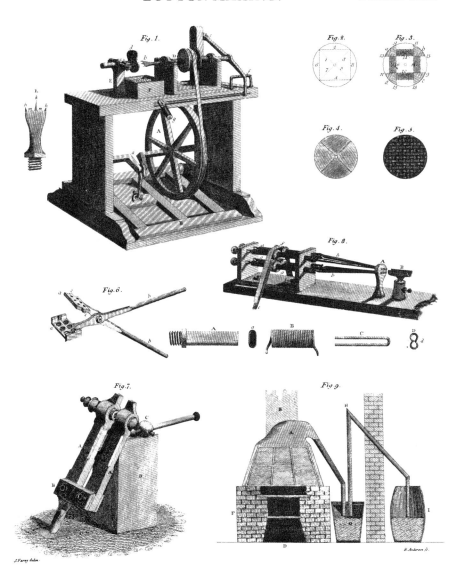

J.Farey delin.

H. Anderson sc.

CHAPTER II

Eighteenth-Century Buttons

THE UNDISPUTED PERIOD of magnificent buttons was the eighteenth century. Buttons increased in size, number, variety, and importance as European fashion copied the French, whose pre-Revolutionary taste for conspicuous luxury overembellished everything. A French cartoon of 1777, picturing a dandy dazzling a lady with the brilliance of his outsized steel buttons, was captioned *"Coup de Bouton."* As significant as the social comment is the fact that the most lavish and extravagant buttons of the eighteenth century were worn by men rather than women. Frenchmen were walking picture galleries, rivaling each other in the number and rarity of their buttons, which included subjects as audacious as "The Loves of Aretino." The Comte d'Artois wore a set of diamond buttons, each of which encased a miniature watch.

The new fashion of narrower, closer fittings of men's garments necessitated more buttons; the already numerous buttons on waistcoats and coats were extended with the popularity of the double-breasted style; and importation of rich fabrics required suitable decorative counterparts: but reasons are unnecessary in an era characterized by excess.

The earlier fabric-covered and embroidered buttons were superseded in France by buttons of luxury materials, such as gold, silver, precious jewels, and ivory. In England, metal buttons replaced fabric buttons early in the century, when, to encourage the metal trade, laws were passed against the use of cloth buttons; however, the restriction was ignored and eventually lifted.

French passementerie was at its height, and the buttons embroidered in multicolored silks, decorated with gold braid and spangles, were the finest fabric buttons ever made. While Louis XIV had decreed in the seventeenth century that the embroiderers in the lacemakers' guild might make buttons of

OPPOSITE: Passementerie buttons on 18th century gentleman's ornately embroidered velvet frock coat, probably French.

Pl. VI

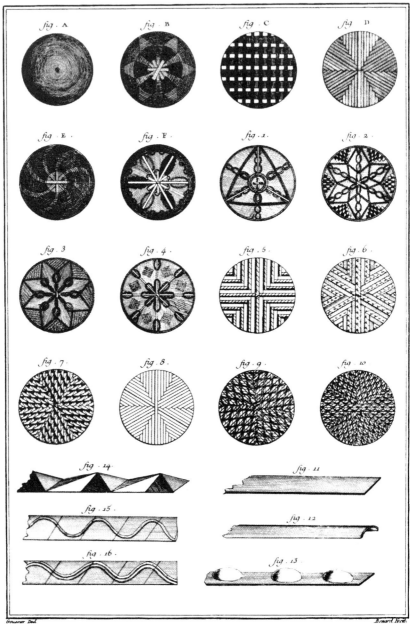

Boutonnier Passementier.

OPPOSITE: Patterns for passementerie buttons. Illustration under heading Buttons, from Diderot's encyclopedia of 1751.

BELOW: French salesman's sample case of passementerie buttons, dated 1780. Courtesy of The Cooper Union Museum.

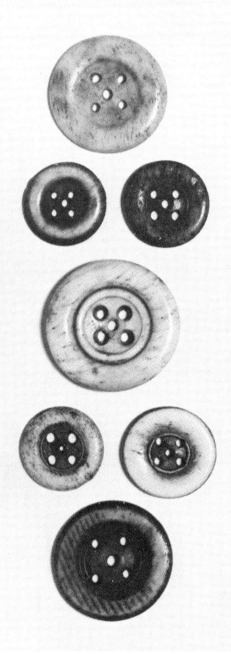

every conceivable shape and fabric as long as they did not "combine artificial with genuine material," by the eighteenth century Louis XV had his own *boutonnier* to assure the splendor and perfection of his buttons.

It seems an unfair bias, which is more likely a limitation of research and literature, to concentrate on French, English, and American buttons, while there were buttons made and worn in nearly every country. Certainly Germany, Italy, Holland, Spain, Sweden, Japan, China, and Hungary had their independent button trades at least as early as the eighteenth century. However, the majority of eighteenth-century buttons, which have been found and catalogued, are from the two leading European button centers, France and England, and from the United States.

Imitations of extreme French fashions and accessories dominated Europe in the first half of the eighteenth century. The tone of French fashion at mid-century can be signified by the *pouf au sentiment* hairstyle of Marie Antoinette and the names of favorite colors: "rash tears," "canary's tail," "stifled sigh," and "agitated nymph's thigh."

With the approach of the Revolution, French costume lost its national focus and was affected by the classical democracies of the past. It was a natural time for the growing English democracy, abetted by the increasing English industries, to inspire a passion for English styles in the last two decades of the century.

English buttons, reflecting life after the Restoration, were influenced in material and design by new inventions, luxuries, and pleasures. Modes of transportation, music and the new operatic performances, exhibitions of horsemanship, animal matches, and sporting events, servants and fine liveries created new occasions for elegant buttons and inspired new subject matter for designs. Whereas French subjects and manufacture were influenced by the Court and wealthy patronage of the arts, with country life equivalent to exile, the English found royal life dull, and their buttons reflected love of country life and the rise of home industries.

Early in the century, French gold and jewel buttons were popular, in conventional or floral designs, or with the jewels used as borders around insets of

OPPOSITE: Utilitarian five-hole 18th century bone buttons. Bone was one of the earliest button materials; there are French records of its use in the 12th century.

other materials. As servants and working people strove to emulate the rich, imitation jewels came into use; it was during this period that pinchbeck and strass, or paste, originated.

Cobalt blue was a favorite color and is frequently found in both glass and enamel buttons. Cut-steel buttons, originated by Matthew Boulton in England about the middle of the century, were elaborated by the French with delicate openwork designs. Boulton also made button settings for the classical jasper-ware medallions of Wedgwood. Toward the end of the century, the discovery of the superior crucible steel made steel more fashionable than precious metals.

French styles and methods were used by the English, whose specialties of handsome metal buttons, beautiful enamels, and fine porcelains were especially coveted later in the century, as fashion influences shifted. English metal buttons were molded or stamped from pewter, silver, brass, and copper, ornamented by designs within the mold, hand-tooled, or embellished with insets of ivory, tortoiseshell, and jewels.

Nearly all natural materials, including minerals, were used in eighteenth-century buttons. Methods of decoration paralleled those in vogue during the century, such as *découpage*, beadwork, *églomisé*, *grisaille*, silver point, silk tapestry, etching, and paintings on ivory and metal. Buttons were painted in the manner of Watteau, Greuze, Boucher, and Vanloo; some few signed eighteenth-century buttons have been found.

LEFT: English blue and white Wedgwood medallion in cut-steel setting. CENTER: Polished agate mounted in gilded silver rim with pin shank. RIGHT: French habitat button, dried insects and grasses in natural arrangement, mounted under glass with copper rim. Three rare 18th century examples.

18th century French millinery subjects. LEFT: From a set of assorted French coiffures and chapeaux, painted on ivory under glass, mounted in silver. RIGHT: From a set of millinery fashions of various countries, colored engraving under glass. The Metropolitan Museum of Art, Hanna S. Kohn Button Collection.

Throughout the century, buttons were made in sets of from five to thirty-five, with even larger sets custom-made for the nobility and garments for great occasions. Sets were often sold in satin-lined leather jewelry boxes, but few complete sets remain intact. More often collectors find one or several of the buttons from a set, since probably large sets were originally divided as bequests to family members, and have been even further scattered by button collectors.

There were buttons, with conventional designs or flower bouquets, hand-made and of excellent quality, which were sold singly in whatever quantity was desired. Rarer for the collector to find are the sets in which each button had a different design but all were mounted and decorated alike. Favorite subjects of these sets were historical events; architectural styles and monuments; digests of hairstyles, millinery and costume fashions; seascapes and landscapes; classical and mythological motifs; insects; and shepherds and shepherdesses. The designs, really miniature works of art, were usually mounted under flat or slightly convex glass and framed in metal rims. At first and unfamiliar glance, a collection of these buttons has the appearance of a delicate exhibit of eighteenth-century art on loan from some lilliputian museum.

A particularly popular theme of unmatched sets was a panorama of earnest cherubs devoted to romance: equipped with flaming and bulging red hearts, liplike bows and intended arrows; in the company of doves and butterflies; softly engaged in pastoral diversions or their work of pipe and lyre playing, garland strewing, lighting torches and fires of love; and finally melting into billowy clouds to rest or survey their cupidic creations. Sometimes, in spidery French script, there were love mottoes around the borders.

Two unique eighteenth-century buttons, primarily French and popular in the last half of the century, were the habitat and rebus buttons. Habitat buttons were made by arranging insects, grasses, weeds, flowers, stones, and shells under convex glass, mounted in metal frames. By the proper selection of flora for fauna, these microcosmic buttons, in natural dried tones of ocher to sienna, are literal preservations of the eighteenth century.

Rebus buttons, following the vogue for riddles, combined words, syllables, and pictures, which represented or sounded like other words or phrases. The decoded mottoes were nearly always amorous, suggested in advance by the delicate and flowery decorative style of the buttons. Rebus buttons have been found with the designs stamped in metal, painted on ivory or on porcelain under glass, and carved in pearl. Looking like tiny circular valentines, they contain boasts, agonies, or promises of love in such inscriptions as "She lost without a struggle," "I suffered for her," "Love you without end."

In the last decade of the eighteenth century came French buttons with symbols and cries of the Revolution, portraits of heroes and villains, and sets of detailed scenes of the downfall of the aristocracy. There are a variety of styles

OPPOSITE: Reverse paintings on glass, mounted in copper, from an 18th century set. Delicately detailed insects with a border of green leaves and red berries.

BELOW: French enamel cupids, probably early-19th century, although design is in the 18th century manner. Cupid with bow, white on cobalt blue background. Cupid with bough, white on cherry red.

of Revolutionary buttons, with techniques ranging from primitive reverse paintings under glass to exquisitely detailed caseins on ivory. The collector must be especially careful in choosing buttons with designs of the Revolution. Many reproductions have been made, since they are popular both as historical mementos and for the typically French verve of their decoration.

The significant costume changes resulting from the Revolution were reflected in button use and button design. Many of those who marched on Versailles in peasants' clothes, fastened by pins, were to become the dandies of the Directorate. Servants began to dress more luxuriously than their previous masters. The foppish fashions and exaggerated gestures of the Incroyables and Merveilleuses are found pictured on brass, enamel, and porcelain buttons into the early nineteenth century.

Against the backdrop of seventeenth-century political and religious shifts, it was natural that American buttons were at first simple, both as a statement against European excesses and for their suitability on the practical garments of settlers. While the Pilgrims, Puritans, and Quakers of New England avoided fancy ornaments, the Cavaliers of Virginia and Maryland imported luxuries from abroad and kept abreast of European fashions. The comfortable style of the Dutch of New Amsterdam, who preferred quality to frivolity, included large solid silver buttons.

In view of British trade restrictions and the newness of the country, American buttons were largely imported from England until the Revolutionary War. The early buttons made in the Colonies were utilitarian and simple in design, characterized by honest workmanship.

With the establishment of more luxurious homes, and as social life increased, there were many more occasions for fashion. American styles, influenced by France but imported largely from England, were on the whole less flamboyant. Yet even in America there were characteristic eighteenth-century extravagances. In early eighteenth-century Boston, then the fashion

OPPOSITE: Rococo paintings under glass, mounted in metal rims, from a set of maidens in pastoral settings. Courtesy of The Cooper Union Museum.

ABOVE: Angels at easels, woven on fabric, under glass, set in metal rims, from an 18th century set.

BELOW: Printings on paper, under glass, in copper rims, from an 18th century set of gods and goddesses.

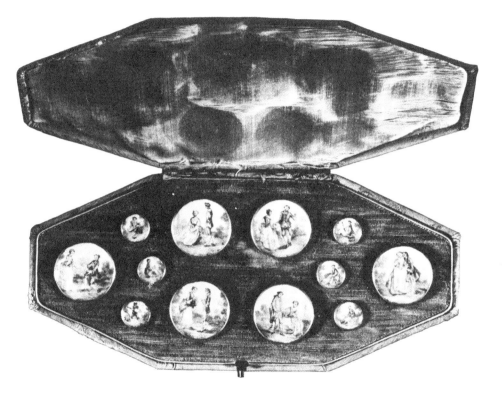

Set of 18th century French painted porcelain buttons, in two sizes, in original velvet-
and silk-lined leather box. Characteristic of sets of the period, each button has a
different picture within a related theme.

French 18th century carved pearl rebus buttons.

center of America, it was reported that a bride wept when her groom outshone her in his rose-pink waistcoat with buttons of dark pink shell in silver settings, over which he wore a silver-gray velvet coat with shell buttons. It was common to order garments from tailors abroad. Elegantly embroidered silk and satin waistcoats with splendid buttons became as fashionable and popular in America as they were in Europe.

Largely, metal buttons were produced, cast or molded by silversmiths, jewelers, and coinmakers, or at home in molds purchased from itinerant peddlers. Even Paul Revere is known to have made silver buttons. In 1770, the master cabinetmaker Benjamin Randolph advertised his buttons of "apple, holly and laurel wood, hard and clear." To reduce imports of metal buttons from England just before the Revolutionary War, the Provincial Congress of Massachusetts recommended the use of domestic papier-mâché.

After the Revolution, the new independence and patriotism inspired an increase in the American manufacture of metal buttons. To compete with England and promote the native industry, newspaper articles encouraged the use of American-made silver buttons with an engraved federal eagle, claiming it to be wearable "for years and for lives." During the last decade of the eighteenth century, individual American craftsmen—some of whom were to found New England button companies still in existence—were experimenting with and improving the production of metal buttons.

Casper Wistar of Philadelphia, who introduced the manufacture of brass buttons in the United States in 1750, is generally cited as the first American buttonmaker. However, buttons were made as early as 1706 in New England, and in several Connecticut towns in the early 1700's, by artisans who produced buttons as a sideline to their chief occupation. Following his father's success, Wistar's son Richard manufactured brass buttons advertised and guaranteed to last for seven years, since durability was a virtue when buttons were used many times on several garments.

Following soon after Wistar was Henry Witeman, who made metal buttons near the "Fly Market" in New York; and Joseph Hopkins, who pioneered button manufacture in Waterbury, Connecticut, which by 1900 was, as it still is, the center of the metal button industry in the United States.

Early American button history can be drawn from inventories, diaries, advertisements, and account books of early artisans, as well as from personal accounts, literary references, and early portraits. Toward the end of the eighteenth century, button factories appeared in Philadelphia and in numerous Connecticut towns. From 1810 there are census bureau statistics and patent records to document button developments.

To distinguish between eighteenth-century American and European metal buttons is not simply a matter of experience in seeing and handling. Often experts cannot be certain of the origin of some of these buttons, since the techniques and designs used were similar.

Sporting buttons. LEFT: Late-18th century English silver. CENTER: 18th century tombac. RIGHT: 19th century English silver.

TOP ROW: Large 18th century men's buttons. LEFT: Stamped copper. CENTER: Copper and silver, engine-turned center with stamped border design. RIGHT: Stamped copper and silver with abalone pearl center inset.

BOTTOM ROW: Large 18th century copper buttons, from a set; die-struck centers, stamped borders, probably English.

Most commonly found eighteenth-century metal buttons are the large one-piece flat buttons of copper, tombac, silver, brass, or steel, with intricate geometric and delicate conventional designs produced by chasing, engraving, and engine-turning. The button shapes are round, oval, and octagonal; the designs consist of hand-punched dots and lines or the penmanship-like spirals and lines of engine-turning. The geometric designs are like exquisitely rendered snowflakes, while the conventional designs—usually flowers, leaves, or stars—have a pure and economical aesthetic quality.

Among the rare exceptions to the simple conventional designs found on these large flat early metal buttons are the horse and rider, suggestive of later sporting buttons, and the prized George Washington inaugural buttons. Made for delegates to Washington's first and second inaugurations, hand-stamped in copper, brass, or Sheffield silver plate, Washington inaugural buttons have been found in twenty-two different patterns, including the initials *G.W.*, the date *1789*, the eagle with a star or sun over his head, and the inscription *Long live the President*. American button collectors seeking these as the utmost button find must compete with collectors of other Americana.

Among the large metal buttons that can be more easily distinguished as European are those with die-struck centers or with variously ornamented center insets, such as enamel, jasperware cameos (sometimes Wedgwood), pierced metal discs, reverse paintings on glass, molded glass, and carved, engraved, and pierced pearl. Around these centers, the border decoration is the same as that on the simpler one-piece buttons.

In the final quarter of the eighteenth century, finely etched fashion plates were the forerunners of the numerous fashion magazines, which were to document every detail of nineteenth-century dress. These pictorial records, along with nineteenth-century patent data and census statistics, make it much easier to identify and date nineteenth-century buttons.

George Washington inaugural buttons, 1789. LEFT: "The Majesty," brass. RIGHT: "Eagle and Star," probably bronze.

Stamping Buttons.

CHAPTER III

Nineteenth-Century Buttons

EXHIBITIONISM IN FASHION at the start of the nineteenth century was more extreme than that following the French Revolution. As extravagances increased, taste declined. Reflecting the general melancholy for grace lost to materialism, Talleyrand said, "He who has not lived in the years just preceding 1789 cannot know the pleasures of living."

Women's costumes changed and blossomed dramatically throughout the century, while men's fashions were modified and less flamboyant. There was a great variety of coats for men, all simpler and of plainer cloth than in the eighteenth century, with former lavishness concentrated on heavily embroidered waistcoats.

Buttons became more works of craft than art in the nineteenth century. For women, the classic styles popular during the Directorate and Empire of Napoleon's Court required few if any buttons. It was not until mid-century that women were to compete with men for decorative buttons as well as for equal rights. Beau Brummell set men's fashions in a simpler, more sedate hue, with his characteristic dark blue coat and large brass buttons.

The quality, materials, and design of the fine metal buttons of the late eighteenth century continued with little perceptible change into the beginning of the nineteenth century. The most significant difference was in size, with early nineteenth-century buttons smaller in diameter, usually about half the size, of eighteenth-century buttons.

Pewter buttons, which had been worn by the "people," had been scorned by the upper classes in eighteenth-century Europe; they were popular favorites in the last part of the century and into the early nineteenth century. In America, pewter household articles brought from abroad were melted down and

OPPOSITE: Die stamping metal buttons from "The Process of Button Making in Birmingham," *The Pictorial Gallery of Arts*, London, 1851.

poured into button molds. In early nineteenth-century newspaper items, pewter buttons were a common descriptive feature on the clothing of runaway slaves and Massachusetts gentlemen.

There was little variety in the appearance and decoration of pewter buttons; generally they were small, either the size of a dime or the size of a nickel. Most pewter buttons had molded conventional patterns, based on star, sunray, or wheel-spoke motifs, often including basket-weave designs, but now and then a flower, set of initials, or an insignia was chased, die-stamped, or punched into plain cast buttons. It was actually the making of the mold for pewter buttons that required more professional skill than the pouring and finishing of the buttons. Buttonmakers usually purchased molds from moldmakers. Button molds, commonly bronze or brass with wood handles, are rare; collectors are always searching for them.

Nearly all early American pewter buttons that have been found were made by various Connecticut pewterers. In fact, three brothers, Henry, Samuel, and Silas Grilley of Waterbury, were the first to start a factory, in 1790, solely for the manufacture of pewter buttons. Early in the nineteenth century, the Grilleys shifted to manufacturing brass buttons, and by the 1820's, other firms followed suit, as popularity transferred from pewter to brass.

The sparkling gilt buttons, first manufactured in the English button center of Birmingham around 1790, were imported by several European countries and America. Outlasting pewter in popularity, gilt buttons were manufactured throughout the first half of the nineteenth century, and represent almost the last hand-finished extra-fine metal buttons ever manufactured.

Actually brass buttons thinly coated with a wash of gold, gilt buttons were relatively undecorated flat one-piece buttons until 1820. Designations on the back of the buttons, called "back marks" by collectors, emphasized the rich

ABOVE: Bronze button mold, with wooden handles, for making ten pewter buttons and a casting from the mold.

OPPOSITE: Molded pewter buttons, ca. 1800–1820.

tone of the burnished metal with terms such as "double gilt," "triple gilt," "rich orange," and "rich color." As excellent in quality as these early gilts were, collectors are more interested in the gilts from about 1820 to 1850 for the unrivaled workmanship of their beautiful hand-chased decoration. Collectors consider this the golden age of metal buttons, and gilts from 1830 to 1850 are termed "golden age buttons."

Designs featured flowers, fruit, grain, leaves, various weaves and textures, and conventional patterns. The buttons increased in diameter and thickness in the 1840's, and were reduced again after 1850, when the buttons lacked the distinction of the earlier gilts.

Within this prime of metal buttonmaking, in the first half of the nineteenth century, the finest European and American brass and silver sporting, hunt club, and livery buttons were made.

Sporting buttons pictured hunters in the field or on horseback; hounds or horses standing alone; and heads or full bodies of game animals and birds.

Handsome hand-chased gilt buttons from the "golden age" of button making, 1830–1850. "Gilts" had a thin wash of gold over brass.

ABOVE: Six gold-plated sporting buttons, ca. 1820–1850.

BELOW: English Sheffield silver livery buttons, with family crests, early- to mid-19th century.

They often came in sets of from five-to-eighteen buttons and either were all alike or had the same border with varying center subjects. Distinct from sporting buttons are the later brass buttons with pictures of animals, hunters, and sports scenes, worn on the voguish sportswear in the last half of the century.

The hunt club buttons were made specifically for hunt clubs in Europe and America. These always included either the initials, insignia, or full name of the hunt club; and sometimes another button was designed for individual hunts, with the initials or full name and often date of the hunt. Most hunt club buttons starred the fox, his full figure running, or the classic fox mask; other popular images were hares, hunting horns, crowns, riding crops, and an occasional exclamation such as "Forward" or "Tallyho."

Livery buttons, bearing the heraldic crests and occasionally the coats of arms of illustrious families, were worn by household servants on their uniforms. Nineteenth-century livery buttons were largely white metal, with beautifully cut die-stamped designs, including fabulous armorial beasts, wreaths and coronets, and almost every heraldic device.

Concurrent with the rise of metal buttons was the popularization of the once aristocratic specialty, the fabric button. Fabric buttons had attained their artistic and luxurious peak with the passementerie of the seventeenth and eighteenth centuries, but nineteenth-century weaving techniques and inventions for mass production of covered buttons made beautiful fabric buttons inexpensive enough for general use. By 1850 their popularity exceeded, and nearly replaced, that of metal buttons.

Generally considered the first major improvement in nineteenth-century buttonmaking was the cloth-covered button with a metal shank. Patented and manufactured by B. Sanders, a Dane who moved to Birmingham, England, the idea was improved in 1825 by his son, who invented the canvas, or flexible, shank. The first factory for cloth-covered buttons in America was established by Samuel Williston and his wife at Easthampton, Massachusetts, around

American Hunt Club Buttons. Not as popular a sport in America as in England, only fourteen American hunt club buttons have been confirmed.

1833. Fabric buttons with the back mark "S. Williston" are rare and highly prized collectors' finds.

Although they comprise a significant portion of button chronicle, and have a fascinating history of their own, there is little collector interest in fabric buttons. An exception is the late nineteenth-century tapestry-like fabric picture buttons called Stevengraphs. They were named after the English inventor Thomas Stevens, who extended the principle of the Jacquard loom by developing a process for weaving varicolored designs in continuous repeat patterns on ribbon. His silk ribbon patterns, including portraits of famous people, landscapes, hunting and sporting scenes, flowers and fruits, were used for button covers. The idea was copied, using other fabrics and designs; few authentic Stevengraph buttons are to be found.

Glass buttons, which began to appear in the 1840's, include almost every form and type of glass, produced by every known process. Endless varieties of these buttons undoubtedly were made in all the leading glass centers of Europe and America, but it is difficult to pinpoint the origin of each. Certainly Italy, Czechoslovakia, Germany, France, England, and America contributed a large share of the enormous output of nineteenth-century glass buttons.

A preliminary essential for collectors of glass buttons would be to study glassmaking techniques and model pieces among already classified glass collectibles. Dating glass buttons is difficult, since there are seldom identifying marks; popular types and patterns were repeated at various intervals, and even trying to determine age by shank construction is not always possible.

English Hunt Club Buttons. Dating from the 18th century, there are a great variety of fine quality gold and silver buttons made for English hunt clubs, and individual hunts.

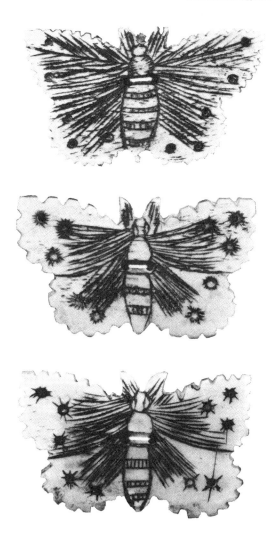

OPPOSITE: Small mosaic buttons, popular on mid-Victorian men's vests and basques, usually Italian.

ABOVE: Bone buttons, considered scrimshaw because they are believed to have been carved by New England whalers in the early 1800's.

Camphor glass buttons, mid- to late-19th century. TOP ROW: Black designs painted on glass. BOTTOM ROW: Black transfer designs, highlighted by handstrokes, on glass.

Collectors broadly group glass buttons into two categories: clear and colored glass, and black glass. The first category includes transparent, translucent, and opaque glass buttons, from colorless to deep shades of amber, blue, green, orange, purple, red, and brown. Of special interest are button representatives of other glass-collecting favorites: milk glass, goldstone, clambroth, satin glass, and camphor glass. Construction and decoration of glass buttons incorporate every possible technique used and any term applied to larger glass pieces.

Black glass buttons, commonly and improperly called "jet," were the most numerous inhabitants of grandmother's button box. If the quantity preserved from the Victorian era serves as a testimonial, and if their uninterrupted manufacture to date indicates a vote of confidence, no other button contests the black glass button as the people's choice. Their history begins with the Victorian popularity of real jet buttons and jewelry. Queen Victoria wore jet buttons on black costumes from the time of Prince Albert's death in 1861 until she died. Her mourning made black fashionable, and the great vogue and demand for jet buttons led to a deluge of black glass imitations from Venice, Bohemia, Germany, and later America.

Glossy, dull, or fabric-textured black glass buttons were made in a great variety of sizes and shapes, using many of the same techniques found in clear and colored glass buttons. However, black glass buttons more often had inset trims, such as mosaic designs or pieces of glass or shell; and more often were decorated after the button was made, by enameling, painting, inlaying or over-laying white or colored glass, brass, copper, cut steel, and other materials. Most prized by button collectors are the few surviving large black glass buttons that have figures, landscapes, or scenes molded in the glass.

Choice among the myriad glass buttons, and a favorite among all col-lectible buttons, is the paperweight button. These miniature versions of the desk weights, which have become such valuable collectors' pieces, are made in exactly the same way as their prototypes, with the addition of a metal shank. One source indicates that paperweight buttons were made at Sandwich. Buttons made at the Clichy factory in France can sometimes be identified by the letter C formed in one of the canes. Paperweight buttons are found in floral, fruit, millefiori, and other famous patterns, which resemble the desk weight patterns made at Baccarat, St. Louis, Cambridge, Nailsea, Millville, and other glass centers.

At mid-century, there were more buttons, of increasing variety and inven-tion, manufactured in more places than ever before. Men's fashions had become standardized in color, cut, and materials, with faint vestiges of button glamor centered in the small jewel buttons worn on vests. Women's fashions rivaled past fancies, often with the tasteless excess and overtrimming charac-teristic of the Victorian era.

There was an increase in costumes for sports and comfortable leisure at home. The sewing machine had become practical for common use, Ebenezer

Rare Stevengraph-type late-19th century fabric buttons, designs woven into the silk, probably English.

Butterick and his wife began to make paper patterns, and nearly all clothes were on the way to being mass produced. An American from the Midwest, Mrs. Amelia Jenks Bloomer, brought her reform dress of jacket, knee-length skirt, and Turkish trousers to London in 1851. Impatient with restraint, women began the battle for emancipation with a few simple masculine garments: jackets, vests, and boots. The new aniline dyes created lurid fuchsias, magentas, and violets, which appealed to the newly adventurous woman.

The success of the First International Exhibition at the Crystal Palace in London in 1851 made way for a succession of international expositions, centennials, and fairs, which promoted industry over artistry. Buttons, along with other items featured at these exhibitions, were manufactured specifically for export trade, losing yet another degree of care and quality to rapid and wholesale production for an eager market.

The fashion sections of *Godey's Lady's Book* during the 1860's indicated that buttons were larger, more ornate, and increasingly pictorial. The small gilt buttons, the silks and velvet-covered buttons, those made of coral and other semiprecious stones, all popular in the late 1850's, were replaced by very large buttons of porcelain, pearl, enamel, and bronze and oxidized silver.

The beginnings of the picture buttons, which predominated in the last quarter of the century, were seen in the spring of 1864 when *Godey's* featured waterproof cloaks "buttoned all the way down the front with large black buttons, stamped with butterflies, snakes, birds, grasshoppers and other devices." Two years later, *Godey's* announced, "The new buttons are exceedingly elegant. The most attractive being of porcelain, or mother-of-pearl, with an antique head in colors, or else a fly so perfect that one feels almost inclined to brush it off."

By the 1860's nearly every country was manufacturing porcelain buttons in their own potteries. While eighteenth-century porcelain buttons are scarce and nearly impossible to place or date, the numerous variety of nineteenth-century porcelains can be somewhat more accurately identified.

Credit for inventing the manufacture of porcelain buttons is given to an English buttonmaker, Richard Prosser of Birmingham, but France has always had the leading reputation for making porcelain buttons. Made of clay pressed into plaster-of-Paris molds, dried and glazed, the white bodies of porcelain buttons are usually decorated with transfer or painted designs.

Black and white enamels, 19th century, probably French. The second and fourth buttons have cut-steel borders. The Metropolitan Museum of Art, Hanna S. Kohn Button Collection.

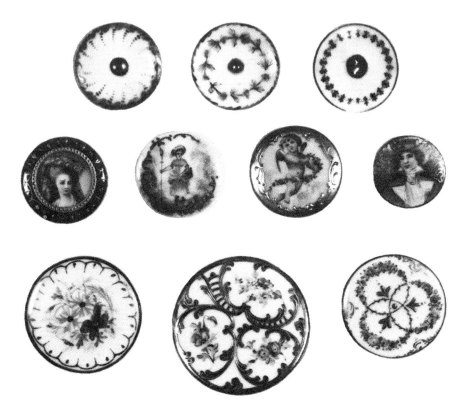

ABOVE: Porcelain buttons. TOP ROW: Delicate floral patterns on glossy white, with pin shanks, 18th century. MIDDLE ROW: Brightly colored Romantic paintings with gold-painted trim, mid- to late-19th century. BOTTOM ROW: Three floral paintings on white porcelain bodies in the style of the potteries of Minton and Sèvres. Center button has silver overlay trim.

OPPOSITE: Transfer design on porcelain with gold-painted background, probably English, mid- to late-19th century. Bird, delicately colored transfer and painting on white porcelain body. Satsuma pottery button with characteristic crackle glaze and gold overpainting, late 19th century, Japanese. Floral painting, border with gold overpainting, late 19th century, French. Painted pastoral scene with gold overpainted border, late 19th century, French.

American so-called "Norwalk" pottery buttons, early 1800's, with mottled brownware glazes, in shades of yellow to dark brown, sometimes streaked with green.

  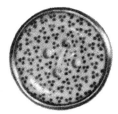

Calico buttons. Small china buttons with designs based on calico fabric patterns. These have white bodies with single-color imprints; the third button is rimmed in brass.

Three more calico buttons. About 600 patterns have been found; they were made in the United States and several European countries in the mid-19th century.

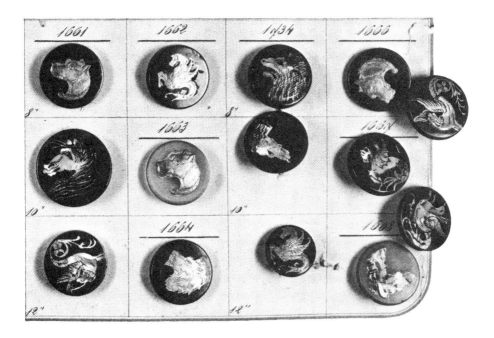

ABOVE: Portion of salesman's sample
card (partially restored). French molded
horn buttons, inlaid with abalone and
silver, real and fantastic animal designs,
late 19th century. BELOW: Brass button,
late 19th century.

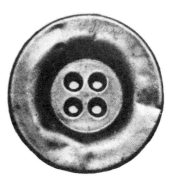

The process of transfer printing is an eighteenth-century invention claimed by three English potteries: Liverpool, Battersea, and Worcester. Most authorities agree that Liverpool was the first to use the transfer technique for buttons, and "Liverpool transfer" has become the term used for the metal buttons with porcelain centers decorated with transfer designs, regardless of where they were made. Liverpool transfers usually have designs of classic heads, but a few flower and bird motifs have been found; predominant colors used were sepia, earthen red, gold, and black, and occasionally soft green or creamy yellow. Hand-painted touches were often used to highlight the transfer designs.

Whether it is the quality and tone of their coloring, the faded near-translucence of the transfer image on the white porcelain, or the usually heroic subject matter of Greek and Roman gods and goddesses, Liverpool transfers have a look of elegant antiquity, which makes them seem to predate their mid-nineteenth-century manufacture.

Molded black horn button with back mark, "Uncle Tom," American, ca. 1860. The Metropolitan Museum of Art, Hanna S. Kohn Button Collection.

Included among porcelain buttons are the rare and consistently handsome Wedgwood or other jasperware buttons; and the Japanese faïence, commonly called "Satsuma," buttons. A very few buttons have been found with black mark imprints of symbols of celebrated potteries, such as Delft, Dresden, Limoges, Meissen, Minton, and Sèvres; these are rare and valuable finds.

In America, coarser pottery buttons were made, such as Norwalk and various kinds of small china buttons. The Norwalk buttons, made in several Connecticut stoneware factories, usually have the mottled brown Rockingham-type glaze and are sometimes mistaken for Bennington pottery. Very popular among button collectors, and usually favorites on first sight, are the small china buttons called "calicoes." Similar, and sometimes identical, to calico fabric patterns, calico buttons are commonly small two- or four-hole buttons (about ¼" to ¾"), resembling old-fashioned ironstone china, covered with delicate calico transfer designs in basic true colors. Very scarce and prized

Abraham Lincoln presidential button, molded black horn, American, ca. 1860. The Metropolitan Museum of Art, Hanna S. Kohn Button Collection.

by collectors are the larger calico buttons (up to 1 ¼"); also uncommon are the three-holed calicoes and those mounted in metal rims. Some calico buttons were also made in England and France.

Shell buttons, popularly called "pearl buttons," had been handmade for over two centuries. At mid-nineteenth century, machine methods—introduced in Birmingham and subsequently employed in the United States—produced large quantities of shell buttons. While they lacked the intricate and beautiful designs of the earlier shell buttons, those produced in the last half of the nineteenth century were handsome and popular; an enormous variety is available to collectors. Of special interest are the shell buttons with pierced openwork, carved pictures, cameos, engraved designs, paintings or transfers when they are in good condition, and those highlighted with gold or ornamented with pastes, cut steels, escutcheons, or other trims. No longer are collectors as interested in the shells from which the buttons are made as they are in the beauty of the design and craftsmanship of the button. Exceptions to this are abalone and the rare cowrie, conch, and helmet shell buttons.

Enamels have always been the aristocrats among buttons. Necessarily handmade and invariably beautiful, enamel buttons maintained their original artistic integrity more successfully than buttons of any other technique, even in the industrialized 1880's and 1890's when their production was at its height. Although associated with France, large numbers of fine enamel buttons were also made in England, Switzerland, Hungary, Russia, Norway, Albania, China, and Japan. Enamel buttons were made using all the traditional methods of enameling: *basse-taille*, champlevé, cloisonné, *émaux peints, en grisaille*, encrusted, Limoges, *paillons*, and *plique-à-jour*. Easiest for collectors to find are champlevé enamel buttons; and rarest are the fragile *plique-à-jour*. Actually all enamel buttons are scarce, and their value is increasing, because even the number that have survived in good condition are being seriously depleted by jewelry makers who have converted them into jewelry. Collectors deplore this trend, since once the shanks are removed, the buttons are no longer considered collectible, even further reducing an already scarce and especially prized item.

OPPOSITE: Salesman's sample card of enameled black glass buttons, Mary Gregory-type, ca. 1880. Inlaid horn button, lower left, is a replacement.

La Mode

27173	27707	27145	27768	37.44
27148	27.46	27149	27147	27150
27871	27872	27668	27069	27108
27712	27711	27722	27710	27709
27720	27713	27714	27715	27735
27220	27221	27056	27057	27732

ABOVE, TOP ROW: Chinese ivory buttons with insets of pearl shell, abalone and semi-precious stones, 19th century. SECOND ROW, LEFT: Oriental lacquer. CENTER: English papier-mâché with pearl inlay design. RIGHT: Papier-mâché with gold-painted design, probably English.

OPPOSITE: Alaskan Eskimo buttons, made from walrus ivory, with scrimshaw-like decoration, 19th century.

Horn buttons, cut from the hooves or horns of animals, had been made at least as early as the eighteenth century. While the early horn buttons usually depended on the natural characteristics of the material for their beauty, or were enhanced by carving, nineteenth-century horn buttons were produced in a variety of methods, frequently with applied decorative techniques.

In addition to natural horn buttons cut from solid parts of the horn, "processed" horn buttons were made by steam-welding layers of slabs of horn; or from the hollow portion of the horn, which could be molded, dyed, and stamped. Both natural and processed horn buttons are of consistently high quality and fine workmanship, and most ingenious among them are those with inlaid decorations of metal, pearl shell, and other materials.

The always marvelous art of inlay is even more remarkable to study on the miniature scale of buttons. Tiny pearl shell, brass, and silver insets—dots and

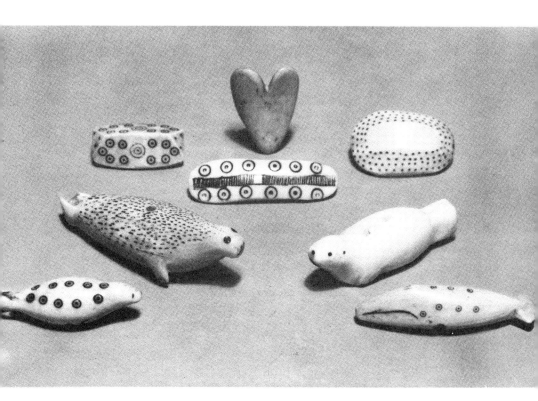

squares, leaves, flowers, animals, insects, birds, figures, moons, and stars—fit perfectly into the molded spaces in the horn. The designs of these buttons are nearly always admirable, but what is superb is the overall feeling of quality— the grain of the horn, the luster of the shell, the shaping of the metals.

Among the most impressive natural horn buttons are those made from the irregular-shaped crosswise slices of stag horn, the rough brown "bark" left on, with sporting designs carved in high relief. Of the processed horn buttons, notable are the molded, usually black-dyed buttons with intricate and beautifully made die-stamped picture designs.

Horn buttons were often dyed to imitate tortoiseshell. Real tortoiseshell buttons, necessarily handmade and requiring a great skill to produce and decorate, were rare. The few that have been collected, either plain or inlaid, are invariably handsome.

Comparable with horn buttons for natural beauty of material and fineness of workmanship are ivory buttons. Ivory was used much more commonly in eighteenth-century buttons, but the few nineteenth-century ivory buttons, which have been found, are of excellent quality. They are usually carved, inlaid, inset, or painted. Italian carved ivories were Victorian favorites, but the

Brass picture buttons, late 19th century. LEFT: Rare pressed brass button of Buster Brown and Tige. RIGHT: Stamped brass with whimsical subject.

ABOVE: Gibson girls, late 19th century.
TOP: Silver button, shows early Art
Nouveau influence. BOTTOM: Brass,
design in manner of Charles Dana
Gibson illustration.

RIGHT: Beautifully stylized French Art
Nouveau portraits, representing the
elements, Air, Water, Fire, and Earth,
ca. 1900, signed "AB" (argas). Buttons
of this period have become increasingly
valuable collector's items.

ABOVE: Medusa. Handsome large brass button with cut-steel trim, late-19th century. A rare example of fine craftsmanship on a picture button.

BELOW: Silver Art Nouveau button, signed. Figure with hair and robe flowing along with curvilinear design.

ABOVE: Typically Art Nouveau romanticized portrait of lady with dragonfly wings, English, hallmarked silver.

BELOW: Brass Art Nouveau button. This was a popular button design and came in several sizes and in various metals.

most beautiful ivory buttons were made in China. One variety of these were made using thick rounded slices of ivory, with intricate insets of birds, insects, and flowers made from jade, coral, tortoiseshell, and pearl shell. The combination of rare materials, the vivid and lustrous coloring of the inset figures in the solid richness of the well-polished ivory, make these buttons ultimate creations.

Obscure and scarce are the wonderfully sculptural ivory buttons, which were made by Eskimos of Alaska and other arctic regions. Made from walrus ivory, looking like miniature primitive sculptures, these buttons usually represent whales, walruses, seals, and fish, or have crude geometric shapes with engraved "picture writing" or dot-and-line designs in black or red. Eskimo buttons were decorated with a process similar to that of New England scrimshaw, which they resemble.

Other natural materials used for buttons in the last half of the nineteenth century included bone, wood, leather, and vegetable ivory made from the corozo, or tagua, palm nut. Vegetable ivory buttons were manufactured in great quantities into the twentieth century; and although their manufacture and history is fascinating, on the whole they were utilitarian forerunners to the plastic buttons of the next century.

Lithograph buttons with paste borders, between 1880 and 1910.

French fashion silhouette, cut-out paper on ivory under glass, mounted in brass, early 20th century. The Metropolitan Museum of Art, Hanna S. Kohn Button Collection.

The leading vogue in buttons of the Victorian period were the various representational buttons, which reached the height of their manufacture from 1880 to 1900. Called "picture buttons" by collectors, they ranged in size from about one-half inch to over three inches and had an enormous scope of subjects. Although they were made in many materials, using various arts and crafts for decoration, more were made in metal than in any other material.

They were worn in long rows, single or double-breasted, down the fronts of coats and dresses, as characterized by the snugly buttoned Kate Greenaway children, who were themselves the subjects of a large number of picture buttons. Flowery Victorian taste must account for the great number of flower designs found on picture buttons. The seemingly infinite subjects included scenes from drama, fables, nursery rhymes, opera, poetry, mythology, history, and the Bible; all species of animal and plant life; every mode of transportation; inanimate objects from buckles to umbrellas; and complete sets of signs of the zodiac. Of pictorial interest, and often of documentary value, picture buttons are not always beautiful or of excellent quality. Many of the finest were made in France and some in England; they were also produced in American brass button factories. Picture buttons have always been a favorite of button collectors. Since it is easy to become absorbed with their subject matter, their aesthetic and intrinsic value are often overestimated.

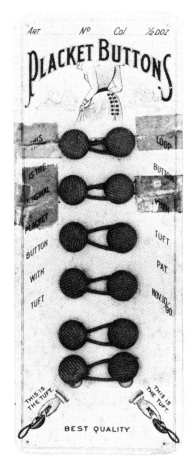

LEFT: Card of placket buttons for bustle closing, with patent date November 10, 1890.

OPPOSITE LEFT: Victorian lady, her basque lined with seventeen small picture buttons, with two matching large buttons on bosom and five on each side of her skirt. RIGHT ABOVE: Close-up of single button from photograph. Copper-colored brass design of fabulous animal on wood background. BELOW: Mid-Victorian veil button, egg-shaped with brass ring center, sewn to corners of veils as weights.

At the turn of the century, the influence of Art Nouveau was reflected in very fine French, English, and American picture buttons with characteristic flowing, curving, and interlacing lines. Often of hallmarked silver, enamel, brass, or glass, Art Nouveau buttons were featured in Tiffany's and Liberty's. Most popular designs were heads of women with long rippling hair, highly stylized figures of women in togalike gowns, and fluid flowers and leaves. Many buttons had irregular shapes determined by the serpentine flow of the design. There were also abstract geometric designs of Celtic inspiration.

ABOVE: Kate Greenaway button, design copied from a print called "Spring" in her 1883 *Almanack*, steel back with applied brass design.

BELOW: "Five Little Sisters," buttoned from tip to toe in characteristic mid-Victorian style, by the English illustrator Kate Greenaway.

Ferrotype or tintype buttons, 1860–1900. Never found in sets,
they are believed to have been worn by men going to war, who
inserted pictures of their mothers, wives, or sweethearts.

Card of men's pearl shirt buttons, American, ca. 1920.

CHAPTER IV

Modern Buttons

TWENTIETH-CENTURY FASHION history can be written almost from memory, with some assistance from the family album and old movies. Costume takes on a new tense: what I wore, what my mother wore, what her mother wore, and what Greta Garbo wore.

The S-shaped silhouette continued until around 1910 when the curves were straightened. The slender, tubular line remained, with subtle variations: it was slit up the sides, draped around the ankles, V-shaped at the neck, and covered by a tunic. The tailored suit and the skirt and blouse were standards through the First World War. There was a philosophical as well as natural evolution from the service uniforms for women in World War I to the school-boy-shaped chemises and man-tailored suits of the career women of the 1920's.

Reminiscent of the dandyism after the French Revolution, strange new fashions were worn by "flappers" in America and "bright young things" in England. Around 1920, buttons with satin "Betty Boop" faces were worn on garters below the knee. In 1925, with shortened skirts and flesh-colored stockings, legs were exposed for the first time; it was the beginning of cosmetics, the beauty shop, and costume jewelry.

Buttons had largely been modest ornaments or utilitarian fasteners in the first two decades. Dresses, which appeared to hold together by themselves, were closed by concealed snap fasteners; they relied on trimmings rather than buttons for decoration. As women's suits and coats imitated men's, buttons began to lose their distinctions; the basic four-hole button, which men had been wearing since the turn of the century, became standard for both sexes.

The glitter of costume jewelry, and the increase of accessories, reduced the need for buttons as embellishment. In the 1930's there was a concentration on cut, form, fabric, and hem-length. The buttonless dresses were soft and almost floppy, while the wide-shouldered suits were tapered in at the waist with a few serious buttons. Beginning in 1932, inexpensive cards of buttons trademarked

"Le Chic" were sold at F. W. Woolworth's. Gay, colorful, and even whimsical plastic buttons tried to cheer Depression wardrobes.

The Second World War only accentuated the man-tailored line, while fashion changes were suspended by wartime shortages. Despite the rationing of nearly everything else, button manufacture in America increased in the 1940's, as wartime developments in synthetic plastics provided an inexpensive, flexible, and available material for mass-producing buttons. Patriotic buttons appeared on red-white-and-blue cards, with trade names such as "American Maid." The buttons pictured, or were shaped like, flags, stars, eagles, anchors, armed forces insignias, chevrons, and eventually, *V* for victory and ". . . –". Reproductions of uniform buttons from all branches of the service were made for civilian wear. In England, blackout buttons, made of white cloth which radiated light in darkness, were sold two on a card: one to wear on the lapel and one on the back.

Synthetic plastic was the new button material of the twentieth century. Made from waste materials and homey ingredients such as skimmed milk, cornstalks and corncobs, coffee beans, and shells of nuts, plastics had very scientific names: phenolic, urea, casein, cellulose, styrene, methyl metacrylate, and acrylic resin. Plastics were sometimes more human than they sounded: when polystyrene buttons turned yellow from exposure to the sun, chemists added suntan lotion to the basic formula. At first button cards designated the names of the plastics used, but collectors seldom make distinctions or classifications according to the kind of plastic from which a button is made.

By 1940, a large proportion of buttons were made in lifelike shapes. Called "realistics" by collectors, they were made of plastic, glass, china, metal, celluloid, leather, wood, sawdust, straw, cloth, cork, composition, and other materials, and were manufactured in every country.

The variety of realistic shapes was as endless as the subjects of Victorian picture buttons. The most popular subjects in the late 1930's and in the 1940's were bunches, baskets, and bowls of fruits that looked like Carmen Miranda's hats. In addition to realistics of single fruits, vegetables, breads and pastries, a complete lamb chop dinner with peas and potatoes was served on a button platter in a 1939 plastic set called "Plate Dinners." Miniature reproductions of brand-name cigarettes, grocery items, furniture, musical instruments, animals, and toys looked more like the furnishings for a doll house than adornments for clothing. Originally realistics, which were called "novelty buttons"

ABOVE: 1913 postcard, a graphic statement of the male view of women's struggle for equal rights through equal wardrobes.

BELOW: Painted satin garter buttons, 1920's. Worn below the knee, "Betty Boop" probably suggested "roaring" possibilities while the policeman said, "Stop!"

by manufacturers, were for adults, but many were designed especially for children. Walt Disney characters were reproduced in realistic buttons, including Minnie and Mickey Mouse, Daisy and Donald Duck, Pluto, Snow White and each of the Seven Dwarfs.

There were many sets of realistics with assorted but related subjects. In the late 1930's and in the 1940's, one of the best-known designers of realistic buttons, Marion Weeber, created for B. Blumenthal and Company sets of buttons with themes such as "The Vegetable and Its Blossom," and a series of nuts and shells called "The Nutcracker Suite."

In 1947, after World War II, fashion was revived with the "New Look" of Christian Dior. As though realistics had only been a temporary wartime gesture to lighten the dreary mood and brighten the drabness of fashion, their manufacture dwindled in the 1950's. The new plastic buttons had largely abstract or geometric designs, with an occasional suggestion of flowers or leaves. Each button style was produced in a range of sizes and a variety of fashionable colors.

The wartime process of electroplating plastic buttons to simulate metals continued, even though the manufacture of metal buttons was resumed. Metal buttons were again made with picture designs. Enormous quantities of buttons were manufactured, even more were imported; button styles changed as rapidly as fashions.

No longer art, with only a few home-studio efforts at craft, buttons have lost both their aesthetic beauty and their tangible feel of quality. Most contemporary buttons are lovely for a moment: their styles do not last, their dyes and finishes fade or peel, they are not saved, and hardly a sentiment lingers.

Minnie Mouse. Plastic, usually realistically shaped, Disney character buttons were sold on cards in dime stores.

Plastic button set called "School Days." Design is cut into button and filled in with white. Made in several background colors. American, ca. 1930.

Mickey Mouse. Walt Disney characters were popular subjects of children's buttons in the late 1930's and 1940's.

ABOVE: American summer buttons. Flag, painted catalin plastic. Heinz pickle, plaster of Paris, gherkin green, originated as a souvenir at the World's Columbian Exposition, 1893. Watermelon, realistically shaped hand-painted wooden button.

OPPOSITE: Button reproductions of cigarette packages. This set is made of paper folded to imitate authentic package construction. American, ca. 1930.

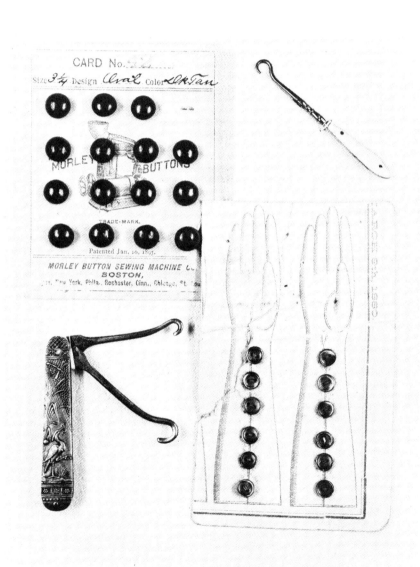

CHAPTER V

Suggestions for Collectors

THE ENORMOUS VARIETY makes it difficult at first to know which buttons to collect and where and how to start. A good beginning is to look at buttons in museums and private collections, find button books in libraries (many of them are out of print), and subscribe to button periodicals. The foremost criterion should be to collect what you like.

Collectible buttons are everywhere, and as a preliminary to finding them, become aware of buttons. They are a nearly unexplored territory, and provide many opportunities for being there first. The numerous costume histories, picturing pages of fashions buttoned from chin to toe, seldom mention buttons.

There are buttons to be found at auctions, antique shops and shows, country fairs, flea markets, thrift shops, and button and trimming shops that have old stock. If not the most adventurous way, the easiest and surest way to acquire buttons is from button dealers; they advertise in antiques and button magazines and have booths at regional and national button meetings and shows.

OPPOSITE: Old button boxes often contain related collectibles, such as button hooks, thimbles, pincushions, tapemeasures. It is also of interest to collect buttons on their original cards, which can be important sources of button history.

ABOVE: Button backs can tell where, when, and by whom a button was made.

These shows can also be good occasions for seeing well-chosen buttons, usually well catalogued and well displayed; calendars of button events are listed in button publications.

In selecting buttons for a collection, try to obtain only buttons in good condition, with an eye to quality and beauty. To evaluate the age and authenticity of a button, turn it over to examine the back for any identifying marks, shank construction, and to see how the shank is affixed to the body. Even more so than with the proverbial things, you cannot know a button by its cover. At first depend on instinct, and later experience will make it possible to judge reproductions or misrepresented buttons. Besides honest copies and honest mistakes, there have been unscrupulous conversions of small trinkets into buttons by the boring of holes or the addition of a shank. To develop the feel of authenticity requires handling and studying good buttons, assisted by conversations with informed collectors and reliable dealers.

Button collectors, through button periodicals and button societies, have formulated a vocabulary for naming and categorizing buttons. Based on analyzing a button's origin, period, construction, and decoration, and applying appropriate terminology from the arts, sciences, and other branches of collecting, it is not a private language. A helpful reference for anyone interested in buttons is *The Collector's Encyclopedia of Buttons** by Sally C. Luscomb; it is an inclusive guide for identifying, classifying, and talking about buttons.

* Crown Publishers, Inc., 1967

Bon Voyage. French tombac 18th century button celebrating balloon ascensions.